CINDY GRANTHAM BROWN

THE MOUSE THAT WOULDN'T SHARE

CINDY GRANTHAM BROWN

CINDY GRANTHAM BROWN

All rights reserved. Except for use in any review, the reproduction or utilization of this work in whole or in part in any form including but not limited to any electronic, mechanical or other means, now known or hereafter invented, including xerography, photocopying and recording, or in any information storage or retrieval system, is forbidden without the written permission of Author or:

Jandy Publishing
6905 Cambridge Drive
White Hall, AR 71602; 479-270-5416;
cindygranthambrown@gmail.com

Copyright © 2012 Author Name

All rights reserved.

TITLE ID: 3990187
ISBN: 1479278022
ISBN-13:978-1479278022

DEDICATION

I Most Lovingly Dedicate THE MOUSE SERIES to my Three Children, JOSHUA, JASON and JESSICA, as they Are My Inspirations for This First Edition.

ACKNOWLEDGMENTS

Authored & Illustrated by Cindy Grantham Brown

Cindy Grantham Brown has authored:

THE RECRUIT
&
"TOPPER"

THE MOUSE THAT WOULDN'T SHARE

CINDY GRANTHAM BROWN

Prissie Mouse is the baby mouse of two big brothers.

Her big brother, Scooter, is seven and her other big brother, Mongoose, is four.

THE MOUSE THAT WOULDN'T SHARE

Scooter Mouse is very smart because he attends Mouse School Elementary.

Mongoose is more like a best friend to Prissie because they always play together.

THE MOUSE THAT WOULDN'T SHARE

Even though Prissie plays with Mongoose everyday she has a hard time sharing her toys with him, making him cry.

THE MOUSE THAT WOULDN'T SHARE

Mama Mouse had to punish Prissie for not wanting to share her toys.

THE MOUSE THAT WOULDN'T SHARE

Mongoose was soon old enough to attend Mouse School Elementary right along with his big brother, Scooter.

THE MOUSE THAT WOULDN'T SHARE

They both were so very, very happy.

THE MOUSE THAT WOULDN'T SHARE

But poor little Prissie was so sad now that she had no one to play with.

THE MOUSE THAT WOULDN'T SHARE

Even playing with her toys all by herself and not having to share wasn't fun anymore.

THE MOUSE THAT WOULDN'T SHARE

Prissie told her Mama how much she wished she had someone to play with and that she would gladly share her toys.

THE MOUSE THAT WOULDN'T SHARE

CINDY GRANTHAM BROWN

THE END

ABOUT THE AUTHOR

Cindy Grantham Brown began first writing stories in about the third or fourth grade. She recalls:

I remember in elementary school around the third or fourth grade, you know, when we were all learning about how to use the index cards at the school library to find a good book to read and how to write book reports. Well, I hated to read. So, I would just read the summaries of the books and make up my own stories. I thought, "Hmmm, if I choose a book by an 'Author Unknown' then my teacher couldn't find that book to see if my story matched the author's." Funny, how a kid's mind works. It worked for me, I always made good grades on my book reports, until the 10th grade when the whole class had to read an autobiography on the same man and write a book report. I knew I couldn't do it and yes, I had to go to summer school and repeat that class in order to pass to the 11th grade.

Cindy grew up in and around Memphis, Tennessee. She attended Southaven High School in Southaven, Mississippi. She currently resides in Arkansas with her wonderful husband. Together they have six children; five are married, blessing them with eight grandchildren. She and her husband are both active members in their church and serve Christ Jesus, as their Lord and Savior.

CINDY GRANTHAM BROWN

Made in the USA
Monee, IL
22 June 2025